Playing Fair

by Shelly Nielsen
illustrated by
Virginia Kylberg

Published by Abdo & Daughters, 6535 Cecilia Circle, Edina, Minnesota 55439

Copyright© 1992 by Abdo Consulting Group, Inc., Pentagon Tower, P.O. Box 36036, Minneapolis, Minnesota 55435. International copyrights reserved in all countries. No part of this book may be reproduced in any form without written permission from the publisher. Printed in the United States.

Edited by: Rosemary Wallner

Library of Congress Cataloging-in-Publication Data

Nielsen, Shelly, 1958-
        Playing Fair / written by Shelly Nielsen ; edited by Rosemary Wallner.
                p. cm. -- (Values matter)
        Summary: Brief rhymes present occasions when fairness is needed in dealing with friends, bullies, games, groups, and tests.
        ISBN 1-56239-065-1
        1. Play -- Juvenile poetry. 2. Fairness -- Juvenile poetry. 3. Children's poetry, American. [1. Fairness -- Poetry. 2. Sportsmanship -- Poetry. 3. Conduct of life -- Poetry. 4. American poetry.] I. Wallner, Rosemary, 1964-   . II. Title. III. Series: Nielsen, Shelly, 1958- Values matter.
        PS3564.I354P58 1992   811'.54--dc20   91-73043
                                                          CIP
Second printing 2002   AC

Playing Fair

Abdo & Daughters
Minneapolis

It's Not Fair!

All the kids were playing tag —
everyone but me.
"You're too little to play," said Peg,
and the other kids agreed.

"I'm *not* too little to play;
just give me a chance — you'll see.
I'll run fast if you let me stay.
Please, be fair to me!"

Want to Play?

My little brother, Benji,
doesn't seem to belong.
He asks silly questions
and does *everything* wrong.
He borrows my toys,
and is always in my way.
But watch how he smiles
when I ask, "Benji — want to play?"

Take-a-Turn

My turn, your turn.
Playing with my friends.
When I give other players a turn,
my turn comes around again.

Our Club

Helen wanted to join our club,
but Becky said, "Get lost!
We only let cool kids in our group —
so get going; I'm the boss."
"Hey!" I said, "That isn't fair!
This club is supposed to be fun.
I'd much rather be a member of
a club for *everyone*."

Follow the Rules

Hey!
I saw you cheat, Simeon,
just for a better score!
A game's no fun
when someone's cheating.
Don't do it anymore.

Test Time

I hate tests,
but teachers love 'em.
Look —
here comes another of 'em.
But one thing's certain —
I never cheat.
My eyes never wander
from my sheet.

No Peeking, Please

When my friends play hide-and-seek
I close my eyes;
I do not peek.
Once I kept my eyes open wide,
and saw where everyone
went to hide.
But — know what? —
that wasn't fun, you guys.
All it did
was wreck the surprise.

So, go on, now —
take off,
run!
Look out, everyone, here I come!

Yuck - Bullies!

I don't like bullies;
they don't play fair.
They call me names,
and pull my hair.
They tell big lies,
and laugh and stare.
The best thing for bullies
is to pretend they're not there.

Good Sport

Who's a poor sport?
Not me, not me.
When I lose a game,
I don't whine or scream.
I never throw tantrums,
pout, or snort.
I'm an extra-special good sport.

Hip-Hip-Hooray!

Three cheers for games - what fun, what fun!
Three cheers for us - we won, we won!
Three cheers from here, three cheers from there.
Three cheers to the other team - for playing fair.

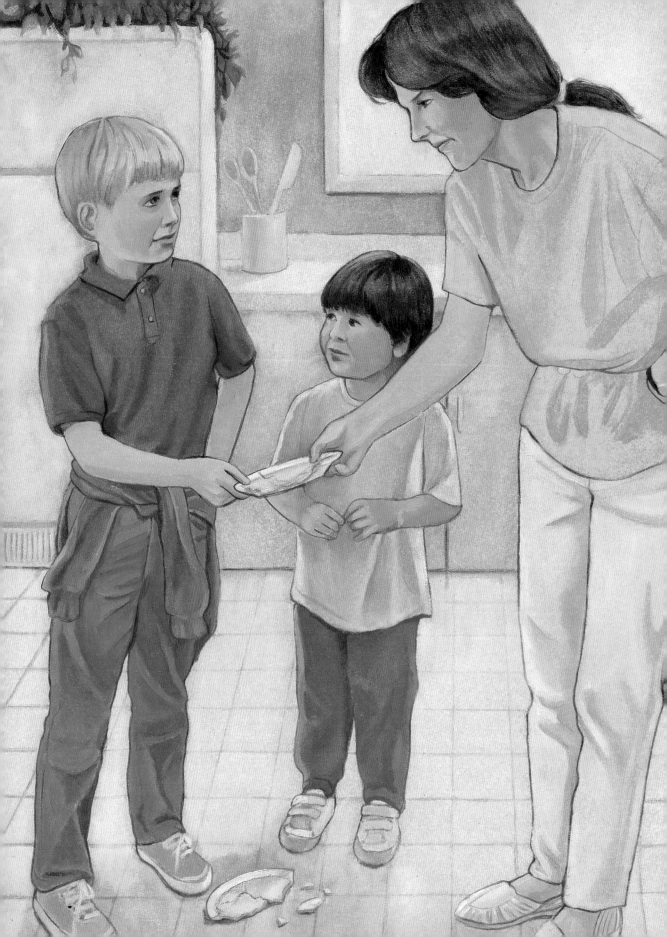

Tattletale

Toby said he's going to tell,
because I broke the platter.
"You better not,"
I yelled right back.
"Cause no one likes a tattler!"
Then I knew what I could do;
I'd tell Mom — just admit it.
Toby couldn't tattle on me
if I'd already said,
"*I* did it."

Terrific Teamwork

Number off —
　　　one,
　　　two,
　　　one,
　　　two.
When we pick teams
that's how we choose.
We don't hurt feelings
by taking best players first;
the last one chosen
always feels the worst.

I Promised

Promises, promises.
I said I would.
If I say I'm going to —
then I *should*.

My Fair Share

At my house,
we all have jobs.
Mom cooks spaghetti;
Dad fixes thingamabobs.
My brother washes dishes,
my sister sweeps with a broom,
and I pick up toys
in my room.
I'd rather not
have jobs to share;
but I do my part;
it's only fair.